NATURAL SCIENCE PRIMARY 4

BY ME

ACTIVITY BOOK

UNIT 1 Body systems

1 Label the organs of the body.

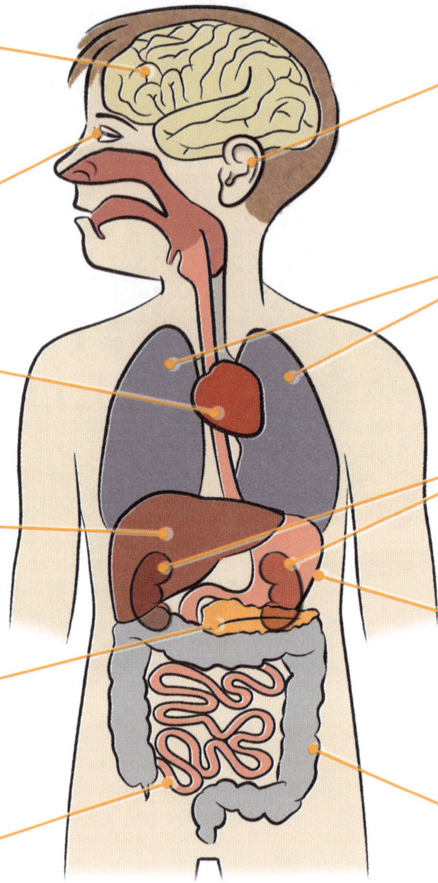

a. *brain*

b. ______________

c. ______________

d. ______________

e. ______________

f. ______________

g. ______________

h. ______________

i. ______________

j. ______________

k. ______________

2 Complete each sentence with the correct body system. Match the pictures to the correct sentence.

1 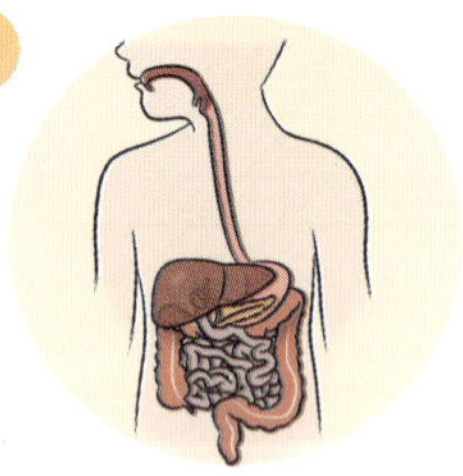

2 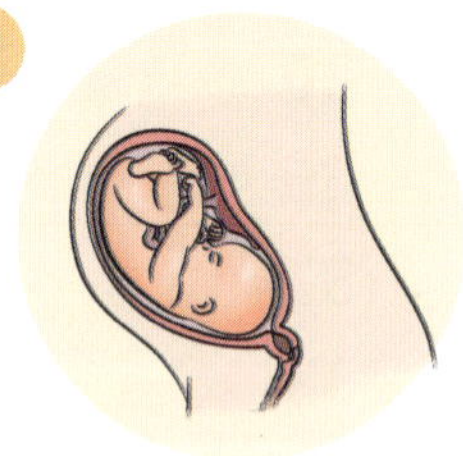

3 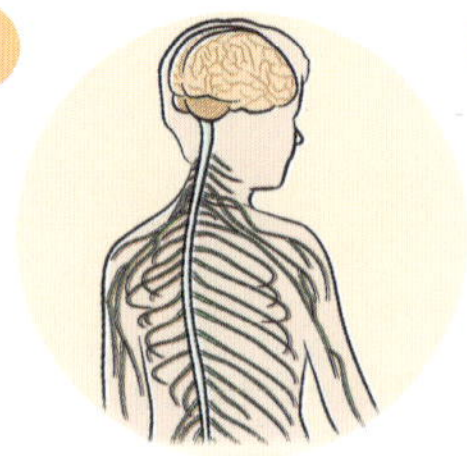

4 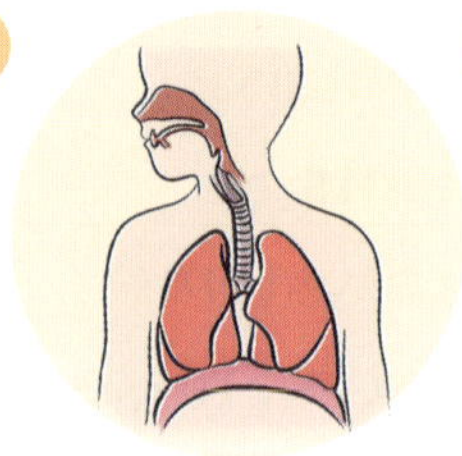

5 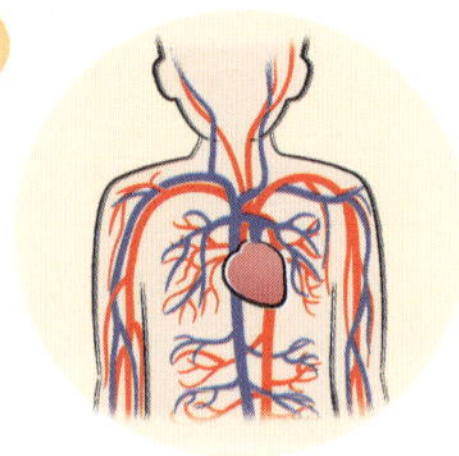

a. [*4*] We are able to breathe because of the *respiratory* system.

b. [ ] The ______________ system breaks food down into nutrients.

c. [ ] The ______________ system moves blood through the heart and around the body.

d. [ ] The ______________ system makes it possible to have babies.

e. [ ] The ______________ system includes the brain, spinal cord and nerves.

3 Complete the sentences about the circulatory system.

waste vessels cells carbon dioxide nutrients heart ~~circulatory~~

a. The circulatory system consists of the heart, blood ______________ and blood. It moves blood through the ______________ and around the body.

b. Blood gives our ______________ the oxygen and ______________ they need.

c. Blood also collects ______________ products, like ______________, and takes them to the parts of the body which expel them.

4 Label the parts of the excretory system.

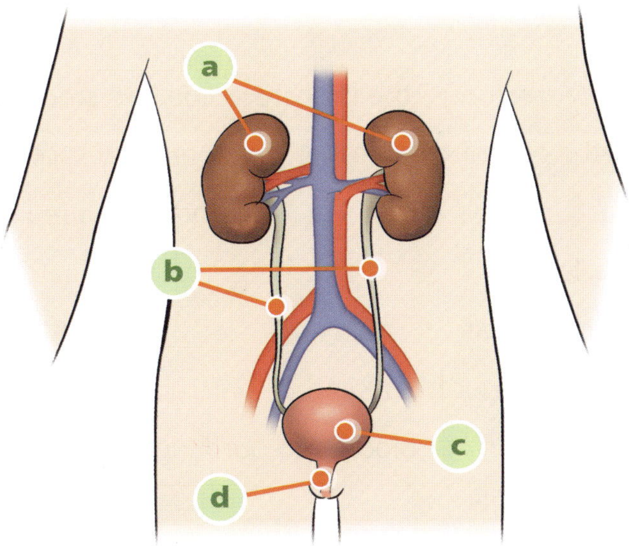

a. ______________

b. ______________

c. ______________

d. ______________

5 Use your answers from Activity 4 to complete the sentences. Order the sentences to describe the excretory system.

a. The urine then collects in a bag called the ______________. ☐

b. Urine travels down two tubes, called ______________. ☐

c. Two organs, called ______________, clean waste from our blood. The waste combines with water to make urine. [1]

d. When the ______________ is full, the urine leaves the body through the ______________. ☐

6 Look at the diagram. Complete the sentences to describe how the respiratory system works.

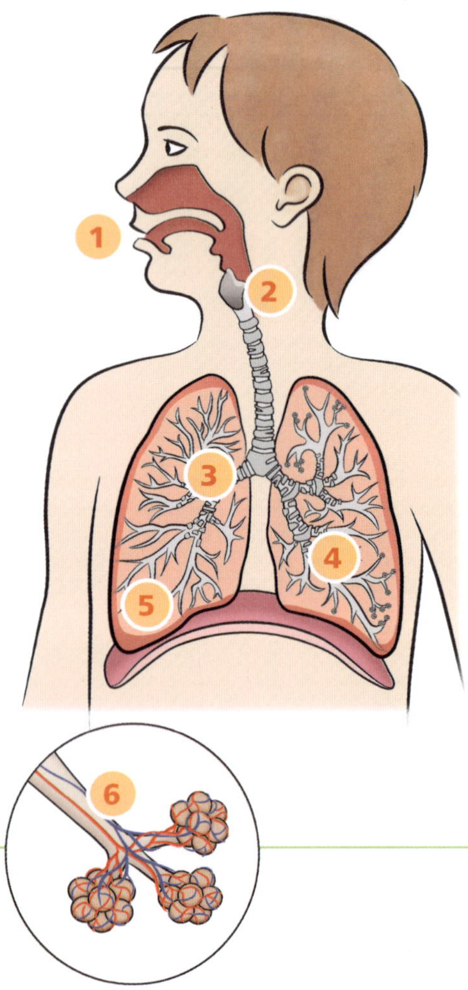

~~nose~~ trachea carbon dioxide alveoli lungs pharynx mouth oxygen bronchi

1. We breathe in through our ___*nose*___ and ___________.
2. The ___________ opens and the air goes down a tube called the ___________.
3. The trachea divides into two tubes called ___________.
4. The air passes through the bronchi and enters the ___________.
5. Inside the lungs, the bronchi divide into smaller tubes. At the end of these tubes, there are tiny sacs called ___________ which are covered in capillaries.
6. It is here that ___________ passes from our lungs into our blood and ___________ passes from our blood into our lungs.

7 Match the words in the box to the correct definition.

~~oesophagus~~ small intestine large intestine anus circulatory system

a. This tube carries food from your mouth to your stomach. ___*oesophagus*___
b. In the digestive system, this organ separates the nutrients from the waste. ___________
c. This is where the nutrients go, after being separated from the waste. ___________
d. This is where the waste goes, after being separated from the nutrients. ___________
e. This is where the waste leaves the body. ___________

8 Label the male and female reproductive organs.

a. ______

b. ______

c. ______

d. ______

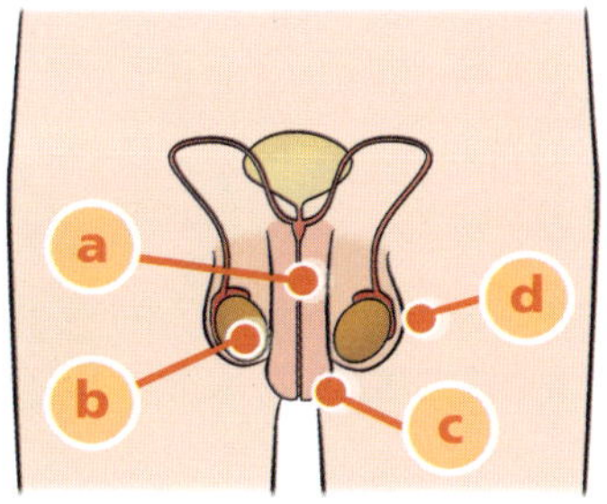

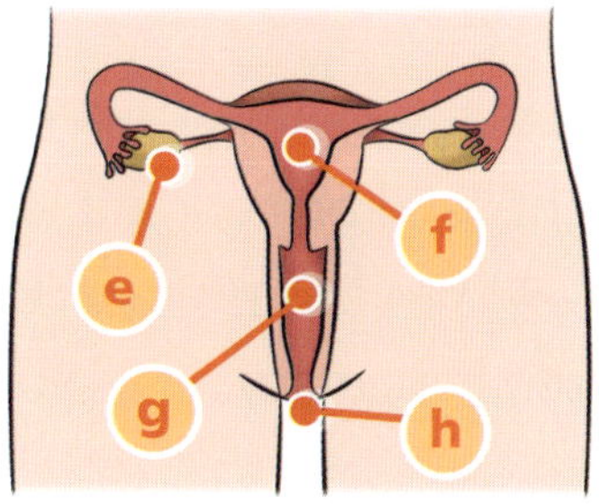

e. ______

f. ______

g. ______

h. ______

9 Identify and order the stages of reproduction.

foetus   birth   ~~fertilisation~~   embryo

a

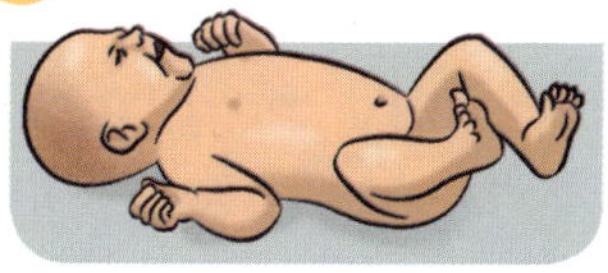

b

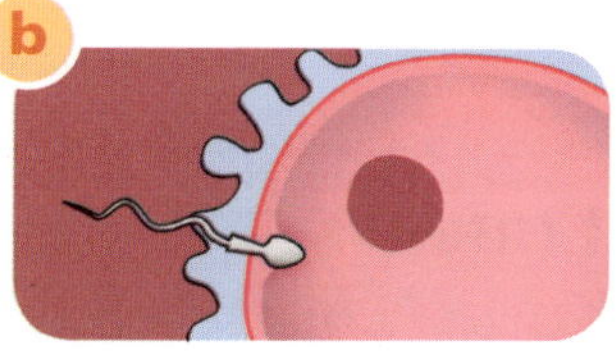

c

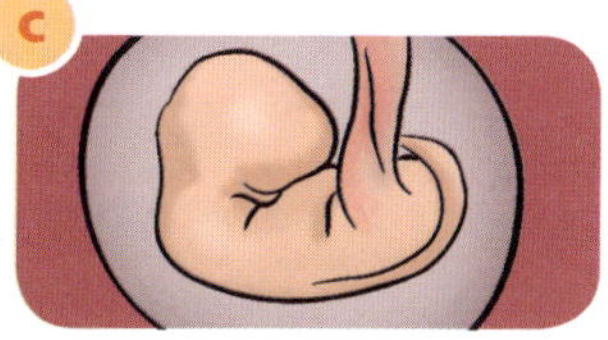

d

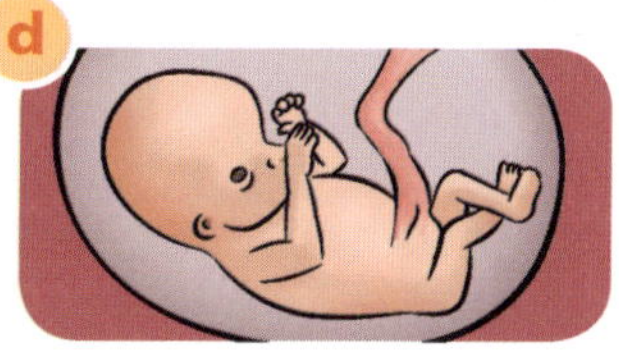

earliest → latest

b	fertilisation
☐	______
☐	______
☐	______

10 Read about how a baby is born. Match to identify each stage.

Fertilisation	The embryo becomes a foetus. Limbs and organs start to grow.
First three months	The baby is born.
Second three months	A sperm joins an ovum.
Last three months	The foetus is developed and prepares for birth.
Birth	The face starts to form.

Find out at home!

1. Investigate how fast your heart beats:

1. Do you know your heart rate? Put the first two fingers of your right hand on your left wrist below your left thumb. Can you feel your pulse?
2. Using a clock, count how many times your heart beats in 60 seconds.
3. Do you think your heart always beats at the same rate? Check your heart rate at different times during the day, after different activities. Write the results in the table. Compare your results with someone else in your family.

2. Complete the chart.

	My heart rate	My family member's heart rate
In the morning, before getting out of bed		
When watching TV or reading		
After walking		
After running or playing sport		

Skills check

1 Look and read. Write some words to complete the sentences below. You can use 1, 2 or 3 words.

Look after your heart and lungs

The circulatory system and the respiratory system work together. Your heart, blood and lungs help transport oxygen and nutrients to all your body's cells. There are lots of things you can do to look after them.

Keep your heart strong by exercising for at least 30 minutes every day. Breathing hard also makes the muscles around your lungs stronger.

You also need to eat healthy food, drink lots of clean water and get plenty of sleep every night.

Finally, it's important not to smoke. Smoking damages your lungs and also causes heart problems.

Take good care of your heart and lungs and they will take care of you for a long time!

a. Together, the circulatory system and the respiratory systems transport

oxygen and nutrients to all the cells in the body.

b. Exercising for around ________________ every day helps keep your heart strong.

c. It is important to eat ________________ and drink lots of water every day.

d. Remember not to ________________ because this can damage your lungs.

UNIT 2 Looking after yourself

1 Complete the sentences about machines we can find in a hospital.

electrocardiograph	microscope	~~ultrasound~~	X-ray

a. An *ultrasound* machine allows doctors to monitor a foetus inside the mother.
b. An ______________ monitors heart rate.
c. An ______________ machine makes an image of bones and organs inside the body.
d. A ______________ can be used to perform microsurgery on tiny parts of the body.

2 Complete the table of medical advances.

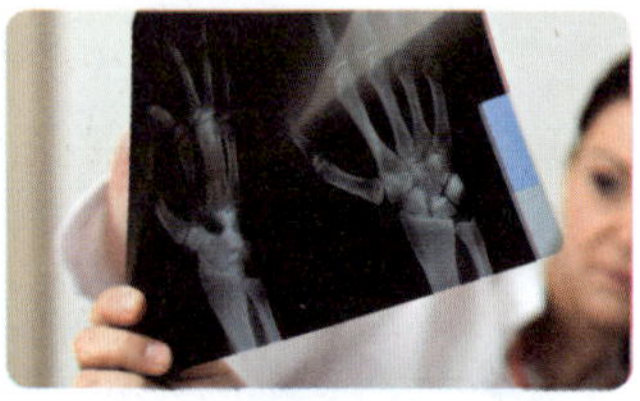
~~X-rays~~

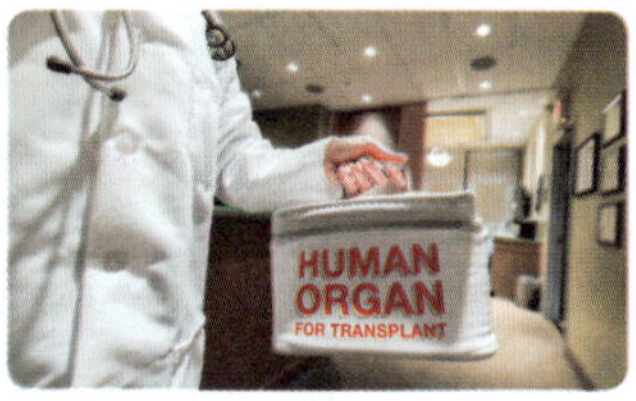

organ transplants

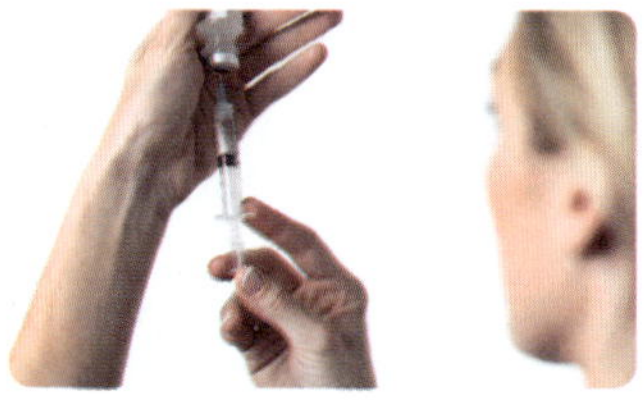
vaccinations

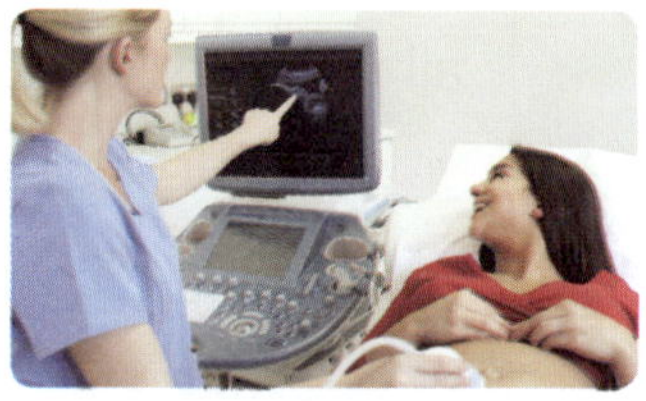
ultrasound machines

exercise

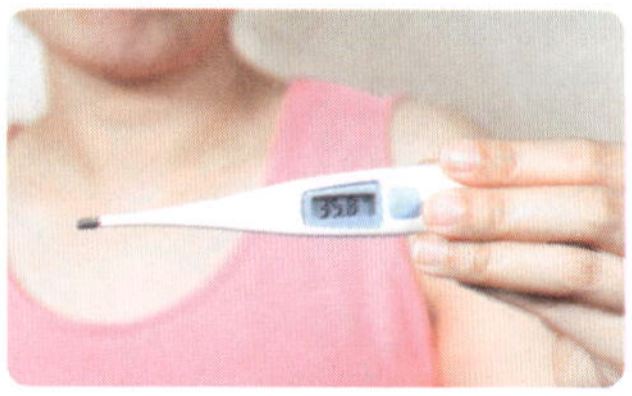
thermometers

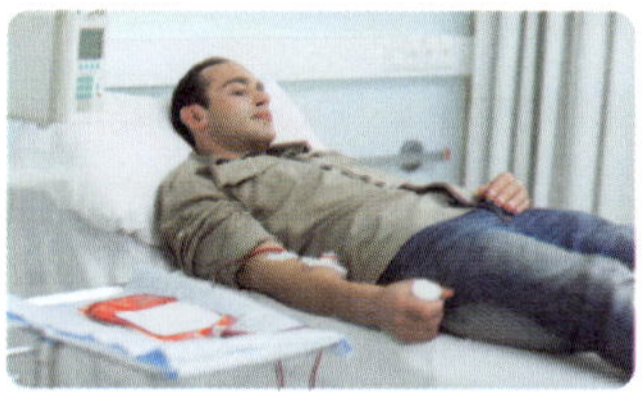
blood transfusions

healthy eating

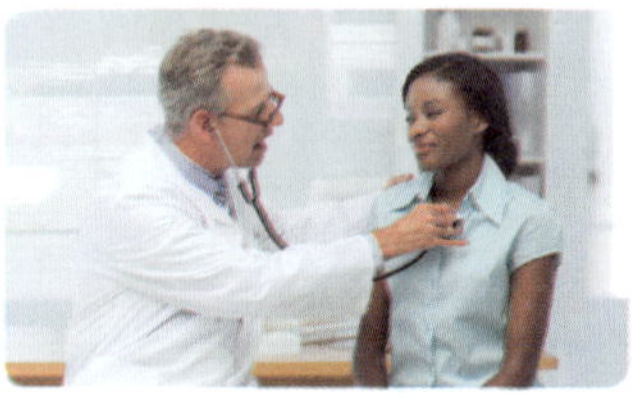
regular check-ups

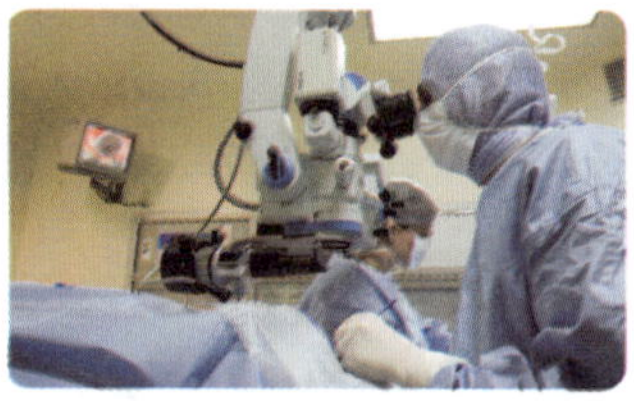
microsurgery

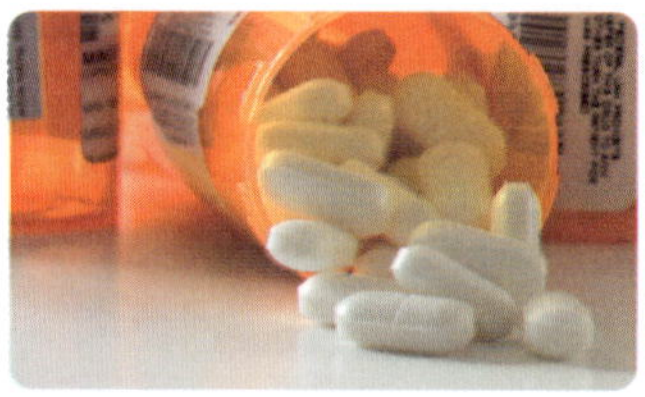
antibiotics

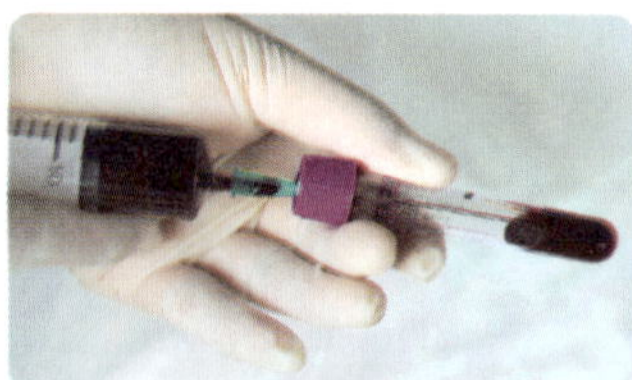
blood tests

Medical advances		
Prevention	**Diagnosis**	**Treatment**
	X-rays	

3 Complete the sentences about healthy habits.

wash memory respiratory brain ~~balanced~~ grows stronger nutrients teeth heart

Rules of healthy living

Rule 1: Eat healthily [*b*]

We need to eat a *balanced* diet. Different ______________ from a variety of foods help our body systems.

Rule 2: Exercise [ ]

Regular exercise helps our circulatory and ______________ systems. Our ______________ and the muscles we use to breathe get ______________.

Rule 3: Sleep [ ]

When we sleep our body rests and ______________. Our ______________ develops so that speech and ______________ function properly the next day.

Rule 4: Keep clean [ ]

We must always ______________ our hands before eating and after using the toilet. We also have to brush our ______________ twice a day.

a 

b 

c 

d 

4 Complete the crossword about healthy living.

Clues down:

1. This helps move food through the digestive system.
2. This helps your heart, muscles and nerves work properly.
3. This is the body system that breaks down food.

Clues across:

4. This vitamin helps strengthen your immune system.
5. You need to drink plenty of this every day.
6. This mineral helps carry oxygen around the body.

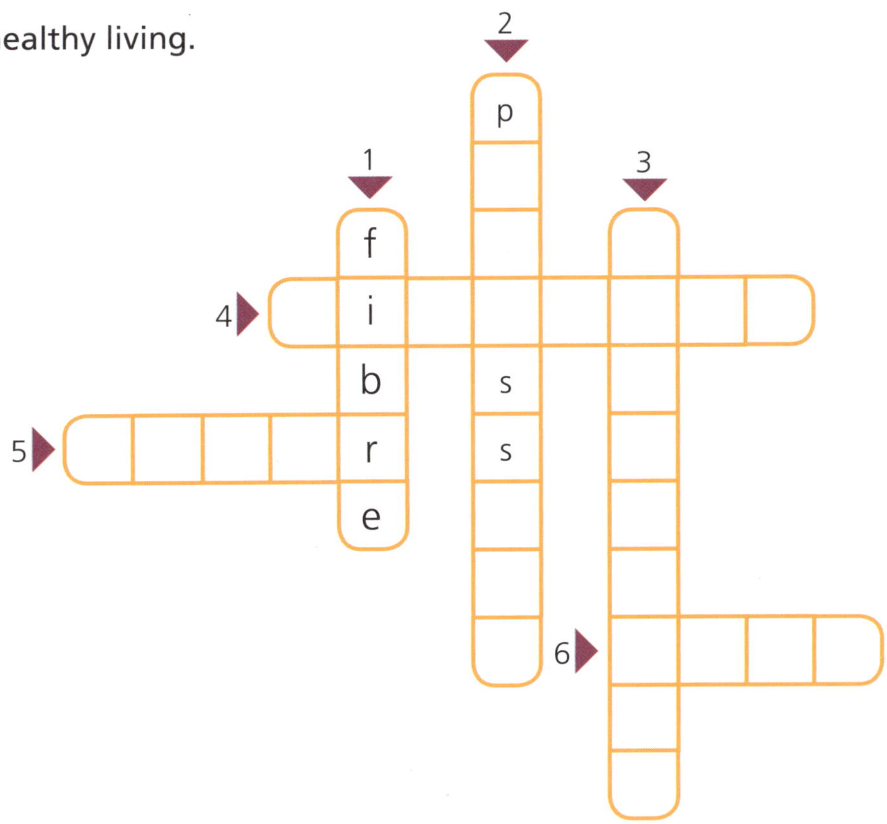

5 Tick (✓) the consequences of unhealthy habits.

	unhealthy eating	video games	smoking	drugs and alcohol
It causes heart disease and obesity.	✓			
It harms your lungs.				
It harms your liver and heart.				
It can cause weight gain, backache and eye strain.				

6 Cross out the mistake in each sentence. Write the correct word or words.

a. Some allergies are contagious, which means that they spread from person to person.

____

b. Some people are allergic to dust, pollen, animal hair and certain people. ______________

c. The body has natural defences, such as red blood cells, to protect itself against germs.

____

7 Read the labels. Why aren't these foods healthy?

Fizzy drink

Nutritional information	Typical values	
Per	330ml (% of recommended daily amount)	
Energy	122kcal	(6%)
Fat	0g	(0%)
Carbohydrate	26g	(11%)
Sugars	28g	(31%)
Protein	0g	(0%)
Sodium/Salt	0g	(0%)

This drink isn't healthy because ______________

______________.

Pizza

Nutritional information	Typical values	
Per	140g - 2 small slices (% of recommended daily amount)	
Energy	407kcal	(20%)
Fat	18g	(24%)
Carbohydrate	29g	(12%)
Sugars	5g	(6%)
Protein	10g	(20%)
Sodium/Salt	1.5g	(25%)

This pizza isn't healthy because ______________

______________.

8 Match and write true sentences about equality and empathy.

A basic human right	that all people	feel differently in different situations.
Empathy is	different things and	deserve respect.
People like	states that	understand how someone feels.
We must remember	the ability to	all people are equal.

a. *A basic human right states that all people are equal.*

b. ______________________

c. ______________________

d. ______________________

9 Look at the photos and consider how each person feels.

a 

b 

c 

a. I think he feels ______________ because ______________

______________________.

b. ______________________

____

c. ______________________

____

10 What would you do to help the people in the photos?

a. ______________________

b. ______________________

c. ______________________

Find out at home!

1. Do you take care of yourself? Keep track of your habits for five days.

What do you eat each day?				
Day 1	Day 2	Day 3	Day 4	Day 5

How much time do you spend exercising each day?				
Day 1	Day 2	Day 3	Day 4	Day 5

How many hours do you sleep each night?				
Day 1	Day 2	Day 3	Day 4	Day 5

How much time do you spend playing video games, using a device or watching TV?				
Day 1	Day 2	Day 3	Day 4	Day 5

2. Write down two things you do well and two things you would like to do better. Compare with your classmates.

My healthy habits	Things I should change
1. ______	1. ______
2. ______	2. ______

Skills check

1 Look and read. Write *yes* or *no*. There are two examples.

1. The children are playing outside in the playground. *yes*
2. It is cold and rainy. *no*
3. Two children are exercising. ______
4. A girl wearing a blue shirt is skipping over a rope. ______
5. The girl standing near the gate is reading a book. ______
6. There are two children eating a healthy snack. ______
7. The pupil standing in the goal is drinking water. ______
8. The boy sitting on the ground has cards in his hands. ______
9. The boy in front of the goalkeeper has short hair. ______
10. There are two children wearing religious headwear. ______

UNIT 3 Living things

1 Read the sentences. Write *living things* or *non-living things.*

a. They are made up of cells. *living things*

b. They have tissues and organs. ____________

c. They can be natural parts of an environment, like water. ____________

d. They grow and reproduce. ____________

e. They interact with their environment. ____________

f. They can be man-made/artificial. ____________

g. They carry out the process of nutrition. ____________

2 Look at the photos below. Write the characteristics from Activity 1. Add extra information.

a

Plants interact with their environment. They react to water and light.

____

____

____

b

____

____

____

____

____

c

____

____

____

____

____

3 Look at the pictures. Unscramble the words.

a 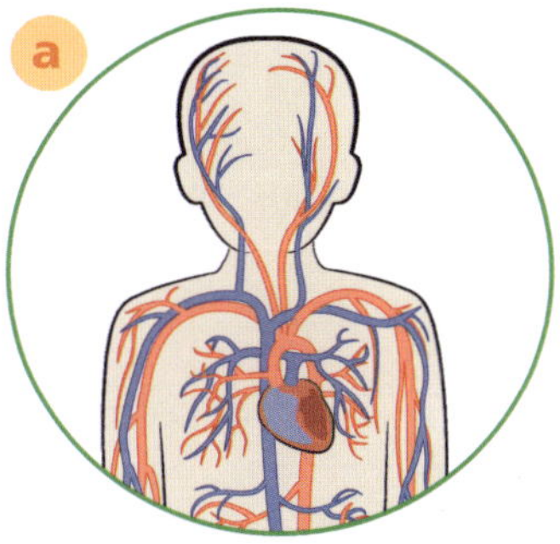

d b o y y s s t m e

_ _ _ _ _ _ _ _ _ _

b 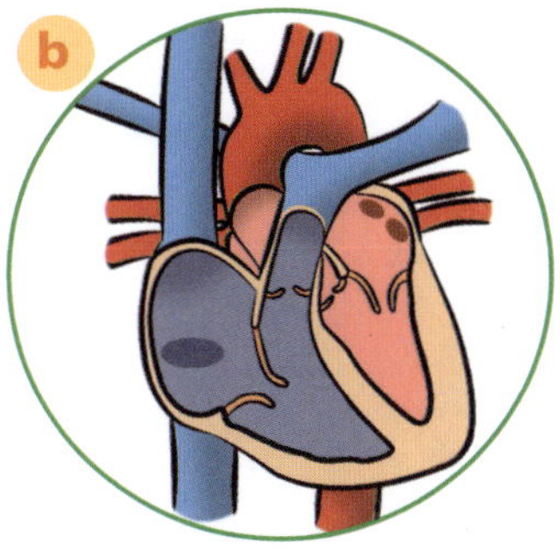

o g n a r

_ _ _ _ _

c 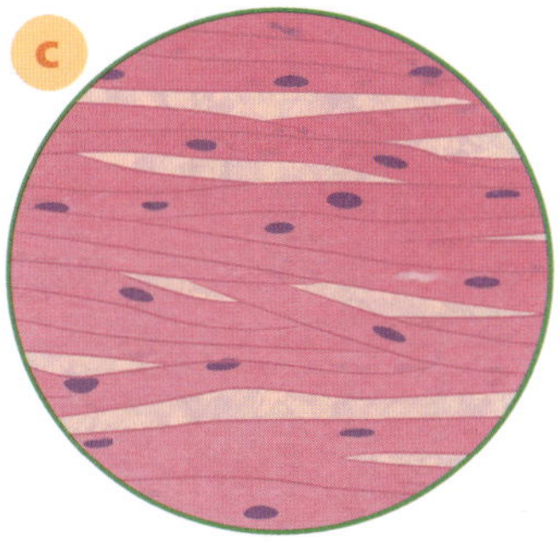

s s t i e u

_ _ _ _ _ _

d 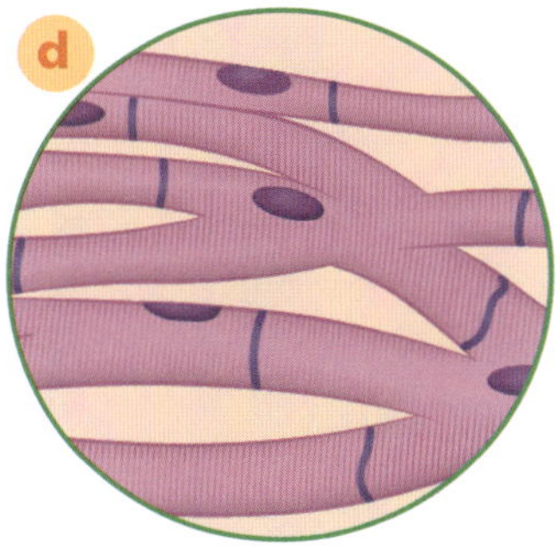

e c l l

_ _ _ _

4 Answer the questions below using the words from Activity 3.

a. Which structure is the smallest living unit?

____

b. What do cells form when they work together?

____

c. When tissues work together, what do they form?

____

d. When organs work together, what do they form?

____

5 Order the structures from Activity 3, from the simplest to the most complex.

__________ → __________ → __________ → __________ → living thing or organism

6 Find the seven vital life processes in the crossword below.

N	U	T	R	I	T	I	O	N	E	S	I	M
G	Y	U	E	Y	B	N	N	A	S	I	N	A
H	J	R	P	T	M	B	Y	M	D	N	A	G
R	O	F	R	W	D	O	S	R	K	T	S	R
P	F	D	O	U	E	S	E	F	R	E	U	O
A	S	P	D	G	T	Y	A	O	T	R	I	W
I	I	F	U	R	D	S	W	E	H	A	N	T
L	E	X	C	R	E	T	I	O	N	C	G	H
A	F	C	T	A	I	S	B	O	T	T	W	I
L	H	I	I	K	C	T	O	N	T	I	T	M
Y	S	M	O	V	E	M	E	N	T	O	N	A
E	B	F	N	F	N	O	C	P	G	N	U	S
E	R	E	S	P	I	R	A	T	I	O	N	C

7 Cross out the mistake in each sentence. Write the correct word or words.

a. Plants make their own food using the process of ~~metamorphosis~~. *photosynthesis*

b. All living things eat with their environment. __________

c. Most animals are viviparous, which means they lay eggs. __________

d. Animals take in carbon dioxide from the air or water. __________

e. Animals expel harmful substances such as sweat, urine and oxygen. __________

f. Animals cannot move from place to place, but they can move towards light or water. __________

8 Write and draw the missing information about the different kingdoms.

	Monera Kingdom	Protist Kingdom	Fungus Kingdom
Cells:	*unicellular*		
Where:		*mostly in water*	
Examples:		*amoeba*	
Appearance:	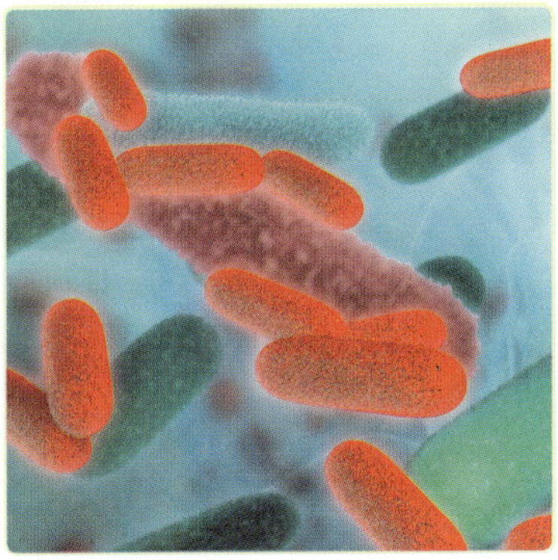		

9 Write full sentences about the Animal Kingdom and the Plant Kingdom.

Classifications:	*The Animal Kingdom can be divided into vertebrates and invertebrates.* *The Plant Kingdom can be ...*
Cellular structure:	
Where they can be found:	
Nutrition:	

Find out at home!

1 Investigate the kingdoms of living things:

1. Find examples of living things that you have not heard of before.
2. Stick a photo or draw a picture of the living things in the spaces below.
3. Complete the case studies.
4. Compare your notes with a partner. Whose living things are more interesting?

Name:

Kingdom: ______________________

Cellular structure: ______________________

Physical characteristics: ______________________

____

Where it can be found: ______________________

Nutrition: ______________________

Extra information: ______________________

Name:

Kingdom: ______________________

Cellular structure: ______________________

Physical characteristics: ______________________

____

Where it can be found: ______________________

Nutrition: ______________________

Extra information: ______________________

Skills check

1 Look and read. Write *yes* or *no*. There is one example.

1. There is only one member of the Animal Kingdom. *no*
2. There are two reptiles. ______
3. There is one oviparous animal. ______
4. There is a lot of plant life. ______
5. All the living things are breathing with their lungs. ______
6. There are people scuba-diving. ______
7. Some of the living things are using breathing equipment. ______
8. We can see members of the Monera Kingdom. ______
9. The living things are interacting with their environment. ______
10. The water is a natural, non-living thing. ______

UNIT 4 Animals

1 Tick (✓) the correct option.

	vertebrates	vertebrates and invertebrates	invertebrates
a. They have a life cycle: they are born, they grow, they reproduce and they die.		✓	
b. They do not have a backbone.			
c. They have a backbone and an internal skeleton.			
d. They are consumers.			
e. If they do not reproduce, their species will die and become extinct.			

2 **Write the correct vertebrate group and match the sentences to the photos.**

a. ____*Birds*____ are warm-blooded. They have wings, feathers and beaks.

b. ______________ are cold-blooded. They are born in water, with gills, and move to land when they grow lungs and legs.

c. ______________ are warm-blooded and have fur or hair. Their babies drink their mother's milk until they can find their own food.

d. ______________ are covered in scales and breathe with their lungs.

e. ______________ are cold-blooded. They live in water and breathe with gills.

☐ frog

☐ manta ray

☐ gorilla

☐ turtle

a goldfinch

3 **Rewrite the sentences with the correct information.**

a. Herbivores eat meat and carnivores eat plants. *Herbivores eat plants and carnivores eat meat.*

b. Animals are producers. ______________.

c. Mammals, birds and fish are carnivores. ______________.

d. Most amphibians and reptiles are herbivores. ______________.

4 Complete the sentences about how animals eat. Match the sentences to the pictures.

chew short flat hooked digested thin ~~sharp~~ chambers nuts

a

a. Carnivores have long, sharp teeth to help them catch and eat other animals.

b. Herbivores have lots of __________ teeth for grinding plants.

c. Ruminants have four __________ in their stomachs. When they eat, the food goes to the first chamber and is partly __________. Then, the food returns to the mouth and the ruminants __________ it again before swallowing it and finishing the digestion process.

d. Birds like eagles have sharp, __________ beaks for eating meat.

e. Birds like sparrows have __________ beaks for eating seeds and __________.

f. Birds like hummingbirds have long, __________ beaks for drinking nectar from flowers.

5 Choose the correct option and order the stages of respiration.

Respiration in fish

- Water enters the body through the ***gills / mouth***.
- Waste ***carbon dioxide / oxygen*** leaves the body through the gills.
- The oxygen is absorbed into the blood through ***veins / capillaries*** in the gills.

Respiration in reptiles, birds and mammals

- Blood cells absorb the ***carbon dioxide / oxygen*** from the lungs and transport it around the body.
- Waste carbon dioxide leaves the body through the ***diaphragm / lungs***.
- Air passes into the ***lungs / gills.***

6 Complete the sentences about respiration in amphibians.

a. When they are young, amphibians are a*quatic* ______ animals. They take in the o______ they need from the water through their g______.

b. During m______, their gills close and they develop l______.

c. Adult amphibians can absorb oxygen and expel c______ ______ through their moist s______.

7 Complete the texts about different types of reproduction.

egg	birth	embryo	~~viviparous~~	inside	live	ovoviviparous	offspring	oviparous

a. Most mammals are *viviparous*. The ______ develops inside the mother and she gives birth to ______ offspring.

b. Birds, fish, reptiles and amphibians are ______ animals. The embryo grows outside the female's body inside an ______, which hatches into new ______.

c. A few species are ______. These animals produce eggs but the eggs develop and hatch ______ the mother. Later the mother gives ______ to live offspring.

8 Identify the parts of these invertebrates.

1. c*laws* ______
2. a______
3. c______
4. a______
5. w______
6. t______

9 Complete the chart about invertebrates.

Arthropods

tarantula crustacean arachnid centipede beetle myriapod crab insect

crustacean

crab

Molluscs

cephalopod mussels gastropod squid bivalve snail

gastropod

snail

Other invertebrates

starfish cnidarian jellyfish annelid fireworm echinoderm sponges

sponges

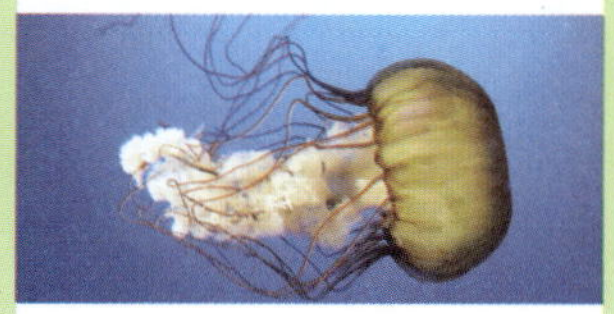

10 Choose the correct word.

a. ***Myriapods / Arachnids / Gastropods*** have long, thin, segmented bodies. They live in dark, damp places.

b. ***Insects / Echinoderms / Cephalopods*** have large heads and tentacles. They live in water.

c. ***Arachnids / Insects / Starfish*** have three body parts: a head, a thorax and an abdomen. They have two antennae, three pairs of legs and usually have wings.

Find out at home!

1 Investigate an endangered vertebrate:

1. Find information about an endangered vertebrate.
2. Stick a photo or draw a picture of the animal in the space below.
3. Complete the concept map.

Vertebrate group

Current population

Respiration

Name of animal

Why it's endangered

Nutrition

Physical characteristics

Skills check

1 Dan is talking to Helen about their school research project. What does Helen say? Read the conversation and choose the best answer. Write a letter (A-H) for each answer. You do not need all the letters.

Example

Dan: Have you decided which animal you want to study for the research project?

Helen: B

1. Dan: Good idea. Aren't they endangered?
   Helen: ______
2. Dan: Maybe I should research the amur leopard. They're also endangered.
   Helen: ______
3. Dan: In Russia. There are only 60 of them left.
   Helen: ______
4. Dan: That's right. So, shall we go to the library today after school?
   Helen: ______
5. Dan: Can you go tomorrow?
   Helen: ______

A Oh no! They are nearly extinct.

B Yes, I have. I'm going to investigate the mountain gorilla.

C No, I'm not.

D Yes. Let's meet after class and walk over together.

E Yes, they are. Humans are destroying their natural habitat.

F No, they aren't.

G I can't go today. I have basketball practice.

H Good idea. Where do they live?

UNIT 5 Plants

1 Unscramble the words and complete the sentences.

egrenever	ndeesle	ocnes	deess
______	______	______	______

a. ______________ trees keep their leaves in autumn.

b. Evergreen leaves are like ______________.

c. Evergreen ______________ grow inside ______________.

2 Complete the crossword.

Across:

1. Carbon dioxide combines with water, minerals and ... to make food.
2. Plants need ... and minerals to grow.
3. Stems ... the plant.

Down:

4. Roots absorb water and ... .
5. All plants have ... , a stem and leaves.
6. The ... carries water and minerals from the roots to every part of the plant.

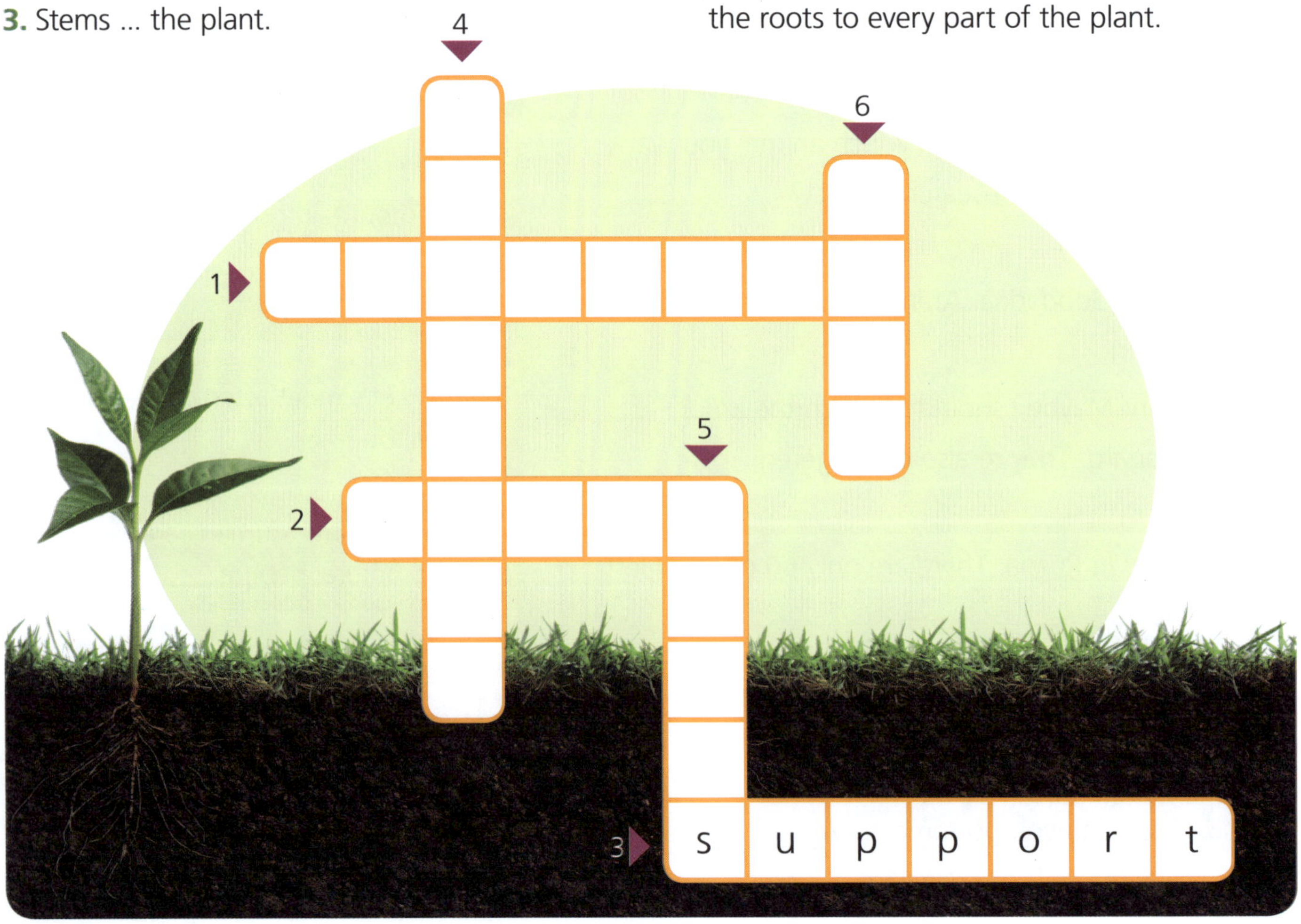

3 Complete the sentences about photosynthesis. Label the pictures.

dioxide	energy	water	photosynthesis	soil	leaves	~~food~~	air

a. Through photosynthesis, plants make their own *food*.

b. To perform ____________, plants need ____________, minerals, carbon dioxide, and light and ____________ from the Sun.

c. The roots absorb water and minerals from the ____________.

d. The water and minerals travel up the stem to the ____________.

e. The plant absorbs carbon dioxide from the ____________ through small holes in the leaves.

f. Using the energy from the Sun, the carbon ____________ combines with water, minerals and sunlight.

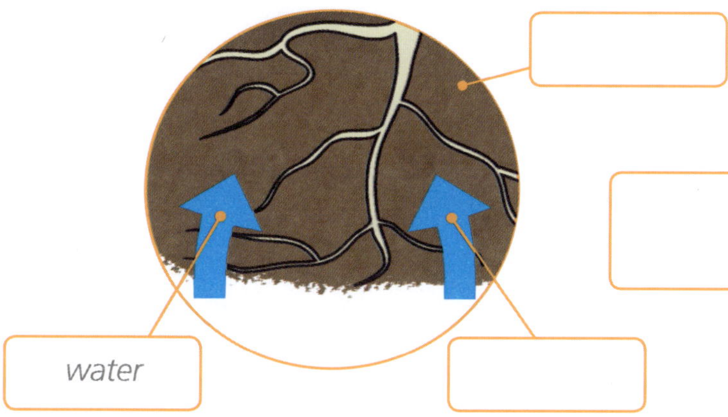

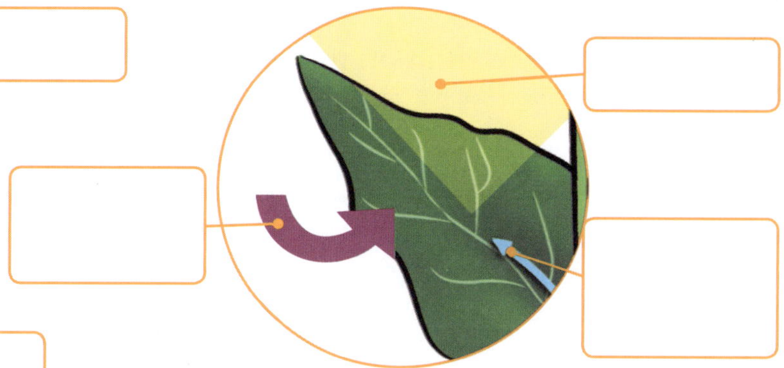

4 What processes take place during the day? Complete.

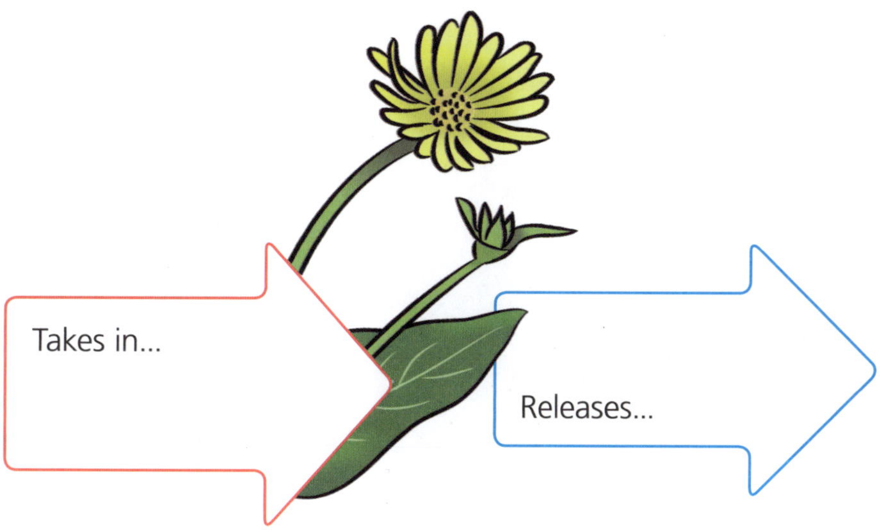

5 Label the parts of these flowering plants.

6 Complete the definition using the words in the box.

stamen	transfer	pollen	stigma

Pollination is the ____________________ of ____________________
from the ____________________ to the ____________________ of another plant.

7 Match and write true sentences.

Pollen	develops	on the stigma.
A seed	lands	the form of a fruit.
The ovary	takes	inside the ovary.

a. ______________________________

b. ______________________________

c. ______________________________

8 Complete the concept map.

bushes gymnosperms trees non-flowering plants ~~flowering plants~~ grasses angiosperms

Plant classification

What are their stem like?

- Soft, thin, flexible and usually short → ______
- Thick and hard, with low branches → ______
- Thick, tall and hard, with high branches → ______

How do they reproduce?

- Do not produce seeds → ______
- Produce seeds → *flowering plants*
  - Inside fruits: ______
  - Inside cones: ______

9 Angiosperm or gymnosperm? Write the correct word under the pictures.

gymnosperm

______

______

______

Find out at home!

1. All plants have leaves, but are they all alike? Investigate:

    1. Draw some leaves from different trees or bushes on separate pieces of paper.
    2. Compare your leaves to the ones on this chart.
    3. Label your drawings as in the example.

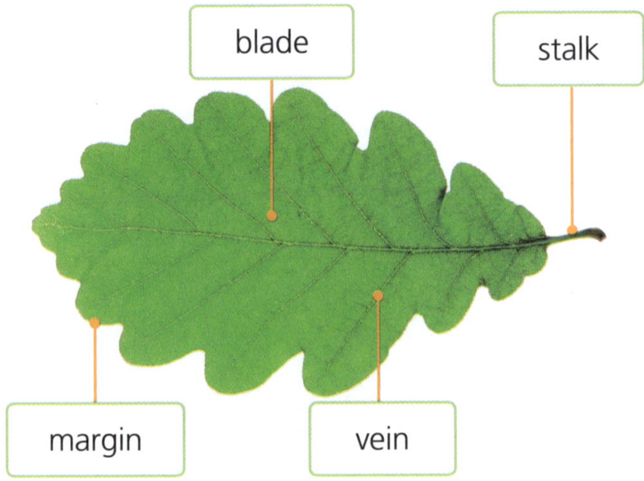

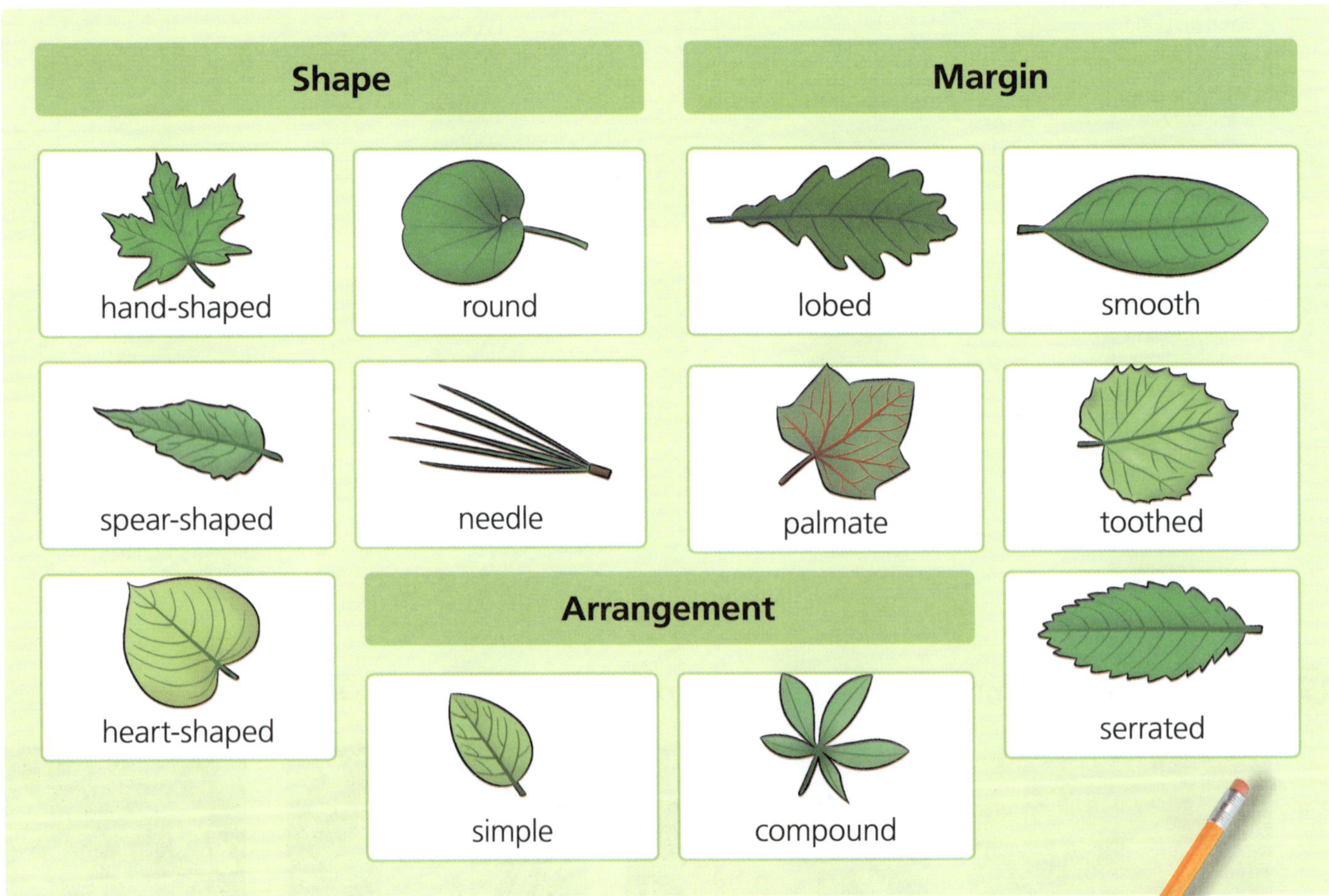

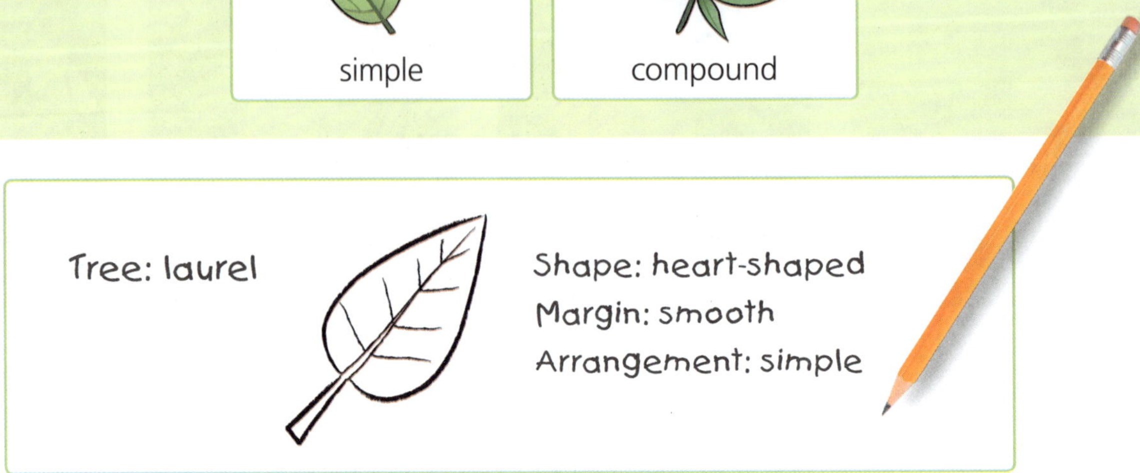

Skills check

1. Look and read. Write some words to complete the sentences below. You can use 1, 2 or 3 words.

You already know that plants are the only living things able to make their own food. However, they are also food for other living things. Invertebrates such as bees, locusts and caterpillars feed on plants. Other herbivores such as cows, giraffes and squirrels eat grass, leaves and nuts.

What you may not know is that there are special plants that, besides making their own food, can catch and eat their prey. They are called carnivorous plants.

Venus fly traps are probably the most famous carnivorous plants. They have a pair of thick, padded leaves covered with tiny hairs. When an insect, such as a bee or a fly, touches the hairs, the leaves shut, trapping the insect inside.

Pitcher plants are shaped like a tube. The top and the inside part of the pitcher are covered with slippery nectar. When an insect comes to drink some of the nectar, it falls into the pitcher and cannot get out. Some pitcher plants are so big that they can trap a frog.

a. Plants can make their ______________.

b. Animals that only feed on plants, such as cows and giraffes, are called ______________.

c. Carnivorous plants trap small invertebrates such as bees or ______________.

d. Pitcher plants attract insects with their ______________.

UNIT 6 Ecosystems

1 Correct the spelling. Match the words to the pictures.

dessert	grasland	forrest	mountan	urvan
desert				

A 

B 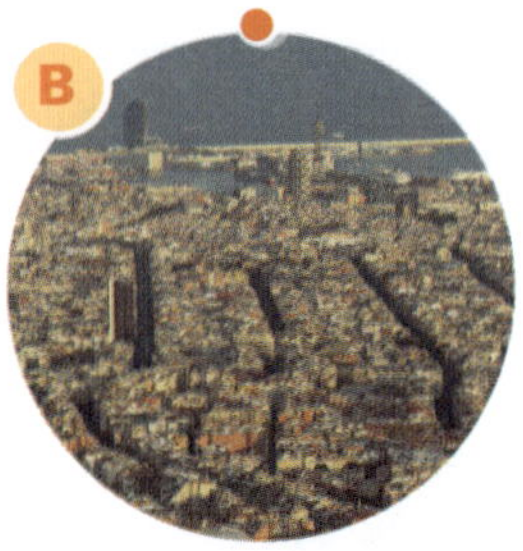

C 

D 

E 

2 Which non-living things appear in an environment? Say why they are important to ecosystems.

a. s *u* n l *i* g *h* t

Sunlight is important because plants need it to perform photosynthesis and produce their own food.

b. a _ r

c. w _ t _ _

d. _ o i _

e. t _ _ _ e r a _ _ _ _

f. _ l i _ a _ e

3 **Look at this desert ecosystem. Draw another type of ecosystem and answer the questions about it.**

a. Name the living and non-living things in your picture.

____

b. How do the living things in your picture interact with each other?

____

____

c. What are the temperatures and climate like in your ecosystem?

____

4 **Complete the sentences using the words in the box. There is one extra word.**

coral reefs	temperate grasslands	savannahs	ocean

a. ______________ are warm all year round and home to animals such as elephants, giraffes and rhinos.

b. The largest ecosystem on Earth is the ______________.

c. ______________ are one of the most diverse ecosystems on Earth.

5 Make a food chain. Draw arrows to show the transfer of energy and label the organisms.

producer

6 Fill in the missing parts of these food chains.

Food chain	Ecosystem
a. grass → zebra → ________	________
b. shrub → lizard → snake → ________	________
c. squid → bluefin tuna → ________	________

Can you think of another food chain in a different ecosystem?

d. ________ → ________ → ________ → ________	________

7 Look at the food web and answer the questions.

a. Which organism in the food web is a producer?

____

b. Which animals in the food web are primary consumers?

____

c. What would happen to the food web if there were no producers?

____

____

d. Which animal is a tertiary consumer?

____

8 Write five things people can do to help stop animals becoming extinct.

1. *We can find out information and make people in our community aware of it.*
2. ______________________________
3. ______________________________
4. ______________________________
5. ______________________________

Find out at home!

1. Investigate three different ecosystems:

1. Use the internet or reference books to research different types of ecosystems.
2. Remember to look for information about endangered species within the ecosystems.
3. Complete the case studies below.

Type of ecosystem:	Marine
Example of food chain	
squid → bluefin tuna → shark	
Endangered species	
The bluefin tuna is in danger of becoming extinct. Too many are being hunted and caught for food.	
Interesting facts	
Includes oceans, coral reefs, shorelines, estuaries and salt marshes.	

Type of ecosystem:	____________
Example of food chain	
____________	
Endangered species	
____________ ____________	
Interesting facts	
____________ ____________	

Type of ecosystem:	____________
Example of food chain	
____________	
Endangered species	
____________ ____________	
Interesting facts	
____________ ____________	

Type of ecosystem:	____________
Example of food chain	
____________	
Endangered species	
____________ ____________	
Interesting facts	
____________ ____________	

Skills check

1 **Read the text. Choose the right words and write them on the lines.**

Fresh water ecosystems include rivers, streams, lakes, ponds and wetlands. They are different (1) *from* marine ecosystems (2) ________ contain salt water, such as oceans and seas.

Rivers and streams are (3) ________ to many animals such as fish, crocodiles, turtles and frogs.

Ponds and lakes are (4) ________ ecosystems. They are habitats to animals (5) ________ fish, frogs and ducks. The main difference between these ecosystems is that ponds are smaller and do not have (6) ________ waves.

A wetland is an area where fresh water (7) ________ the soil. Sometimes the soil is covered with water all year (8) ________. Wetlands are home to a rich diversity of birds.

1. in	from	with
2. that	who	when
3. houses	home	life
4. similar	same	similarly
5. that	such	like
6. some	any	no
7. covers	cover	covered
8. entire	round	around

UNIT 7 Matter, materials and forces

1 Complete the concept map using the words in the box.

~~matter~~	cannot	materials	gas	state	solid	change	liquid	destroyed

The Universe is made up of *matter*.

Matter has three states:

____

____

____

Matter makes up different ________________.

Matter ____________ be created or ____________; it can only ____________ from one form or ____________ to another.

2 Identify the natural and manufactured materials.

sand

☑ natural
☐ manufactured

plastic

☐ natural
☐ manufactured

wood

☐ natural
☐ manufactured

glass

☐ natural
☐ manufactured

crude oil

☐ natural
☐ manufactured

paper

☐ natural
☐ manufactured

3 Find the properties of materials. Use them to complete the sentences.

N	O	N	E	L	A	S	T	I	C	R
E	E	L	A	R	R	E	S	T	Y	F
L	R	E	S	I	S	T	A	N	T	R
A	I	O	A	G	R	N	T	S	E	A
S	S	P	E	I	R	E	P	S	N	G
T	E	A	R	D	A	E	L	B	I	I
I	R	A	N	S	C	A	R	E	N	L
C	E	O	P	A	Q	U	E	U	A	E
T	R	A	N	S	P	A	R	E	N	T

a. An elastic material will change back to its original shape when the force stops.

b. A ________-________ material will keep its new shape when the force stops.

c. We cannot see through an ________ material.

d. We can see through a ________ material.

e. A ________ material is very strong.

f. A ________ material is easy to break.

g. A ________ material cannot be bent.

4 Look at the photos below and answer the questions.

a

b

c

d

1. Which photo shows a reversible physical change?

____

2. Which photo shows an irreversible physical change?

____

3. Which photo shows the chemical change of putrefaction?

____

4. Which photo shows the chemical change when metal reacts with oxygen and water? What is this process called?

____

5 Complete the sentences about mass and volume.

space	grams	millilitres	~~matter~~

a. Mass is the amount of ___*matter*___ something contains.

b. Mass is measured in ________________.

c. Volume is the amount of ________________ something occupies.

d. We can measure volume in ________________.

6 Look at the photos and write *mass* or *volume.*

a

500 g

b

500 g

a. The box of cereal and the ear of corn have the same ________________.

b. The box of cereal has a greater ________________ than the ear of corn.

c. The football has less ________________ than the bowling ball.

d. The football and the bowling ball have the same ________________.

c

450 g

d

4 500 g

7 Add a tick (✓) or a cross (✗) for three states of matter.

States of matter	Have a definite volume	Have a definite shape
Gases 	✗	
Liquids 		
Solids 		

8 **Complete the sentences about mass and volume.**

a. To calculate the density of an object we divide its ***mass / volume*** by its ***mass / volume***.

b. Objects that float have a ***lower / higher*** density than water.

c. Objects that sink have a ***lower / higher*** density than water.

9 **Identify the forces. Circle contact or non-contact force.**

gravity	magnetism	~~buoyancy~~	friction

a

buoyancy

(contact force)

non-contact force

b

contact force

non-contact force

c

contact force

non-contact force

d

contact force

non-contact force

10 **Cross out the mistake in each sentence. Write the correct word or words.**

a. Gravity is a force that ~~repels~~ objects towards each other. *attracts*

b. Small bodies, such as planets, have a stronger gravitational force. ________

c. Friction makes objects fall to the ground. ________

d. Magnets have two poles which attract plastic objects. ________

e. The north poles of two different magnets will attract each other. ________

f. Magnetism is the force that exists when two objects rub against each other. ________

g. Friction acts in the same direction to the direction of movement. ________

h. Buoyancy is a downward force which acts in the opposite direction to gravity on objects immersed in a liquid. ________

Find out at home!

1. Investigate friction:

1. Make a ramp for a toy car. You can use a book or a piece of wood.
2. Let the car roll down the ramp. Observe how fast and far it goes.
3. Put a piece of paper towel on the ramp and let the car roll down. Does the speed change?
4. Put a towel on the ramp and let the car roll down again. Does the car reach the bottom of the ramp? Complete the chart below.

Surface	Observations

2. Answer the questions.

a. On which surface did the car go the fastest and the farthest? ____________

b. On which surface did the car travel the shortest distance? ____________

c. Which force makes the car go down the ramp? ____________

d. Which force made the car go slower or travel less distance? ____________

Skills check

1. Look at the signs. Write the correct letter next to each question.

A

B

C

D

E

F

G

H

Example: Do not litter. _B_

1. Be careful when you walk here. ______
2. You cannot use your camera. ______
3. Remember to wash your hands. ______
4. You have to wear a protective hat. ______
5. You must not run in this area. ______
6. You cannot drink the water here. ______

Energy

1. What types of energy are being produced in the photos?

sound energy

2. What other things produce these types of energy? Complete the table.

sound energy		
violin	*barbecue*	*light bulb*
bikes	*microwave*	*petrol*

3 Match and write true sentences about light energy.

Light is the fastest form	of seven different colours: red, orange, yellow, green, blue, indigo and violet.
Light from the Sun is made up	of energy. It travels at about 300 000 km per second.
Light travels in all directions	behave differently, depending on the surface it hits.
When something gets in its way, light can	from its source. One light bulb can light an entire room.

a. *Light is the fastest form of energy. It travels at about 300 000 km per second.*

b. ______

c. ______

d. ______

4 Write sentences about light energy which contain the following information:

a. transparent

Light passes through transparent materials. These materials do not scatter the light so we can see the image clearly.

b. opaque

______

c. translucent

______

d. eight minutes

______

5 Complete the tables.

heat conductors	heat insulators
iron	

6 Complete the sentences about thermal energy using the words in the box.

0°C	100°C	~~thermal~~	water	state

a. When we heat an object, we are increasing its temperature, as well as its amount of *thermal* energy.

b. A change in the thermal energy of a substance can change its ________________.

c. If we heat ice to a temperature of ________________ or higher, it will change into ________________.

d. If we heat water to a temperature of ________________ or higher, it will become steam.

7 Label the different characteristics of sound. Match the definitions to the correct picture.

a

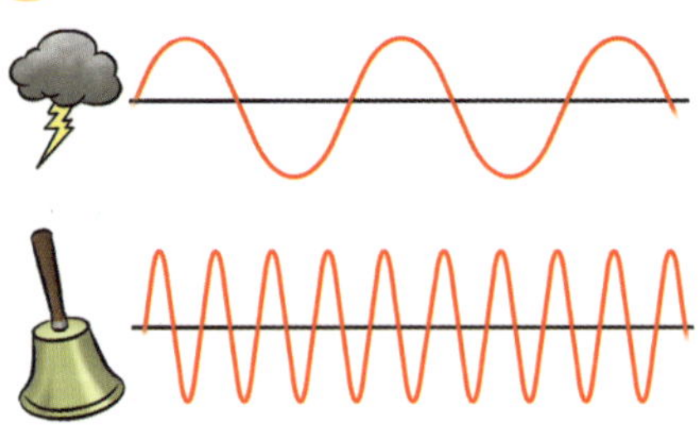

____

b

____

c

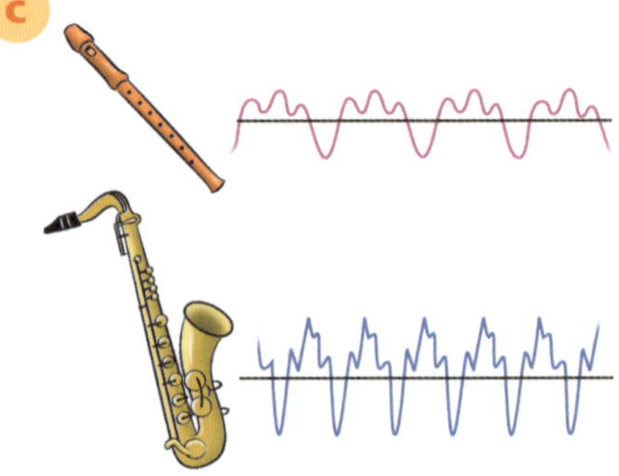

____

Definitions

1. This is how we identify the source of a sound. ☐

2. This depends on the strength of the vibrations that produce the sound. ☐

3. This depends on how quickly the vibrations are produced. ☐

8 Complete the sentences about sound energy. Match the sentences to the correct picture.

sonic boom | reflect | air | changes | ~~directions~~ | solid

1. Sound travels in all *directions* from its source.
2. It can travel through __________, opaque objects.
3. Sound can __________ off an object. If the object is far away, we hear an echo.
4. It cannot travel when there is no __________.
5. Sound can produce __________ in other objects.
6. When an object travels faster than the speed of sound, it produces a __________.

a
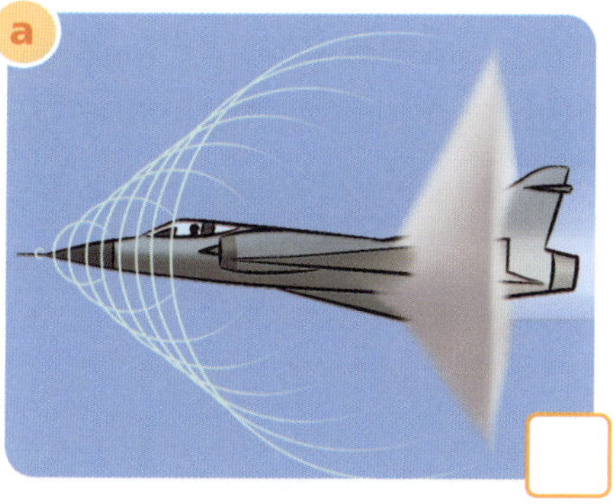

b

c

d

e

1

f

9 Do these sentences apply to light, sound or thermal energy?

a. We can change the state of an object by increasing or decreasing this type of energy.

____

b. This is the fastest form of energy. Most of this energy comes from the Sun. __________

c. This type of energy is produced when objects vibrate. Vibrations move through the air in waves.

____

Find out at home!

1 Investigate non-renewable energy:

1. Discuss with a partner why you think finding out about non-renewable energy is a good idea.
2. Use the internet or reference books to research one type of non-renewable energy.
3. Answer the questions below. Compare your answers with a class member who researched a different type of non-renewable energy.

Did you know that most of our electricity comes from power stations that use fossil fuels to generate electricity? The three fossil fuels are coal, oil and gas. They are non-renewable energy sources that will eventually, one day, run out. They also contribute to global warming; this is the gradual increase of the Earth's temperature.

Type of non-renewable energy	
What is it used for?	
How many people around the world use it every day?	
Which country uses it the most?	
How do we get it?	
What are its advantages and disadvantages?	

Skills check

1 Read the text. Choose the right words and write them on the lines.

Burning fossil fuels produces greenhouse gases. These gases, such as carbon dioxide, (1) ___water___ vapour and methane trap energy (2) ________ the Sun. As a result, the Earth's (3) ________ gradually increases. This (4) ________ increase of the Earth's temperature is called global warming.

There are lots of bad things that could happen because (5) ________ global warming. Some plants and animals may (6) ________ extinct because of the heat.

There are ways that we can help (7) ________ greenhouse gases and stop global warming, such as walking to school and turning lights (8) ________ when we leave a room.

1. gas	~~water~~	wind
2. from	in	near
3. temperature	core	life
4. fast	rapid	gradual
5. in	that	of
6. become	became	have become
7. to	reduce	reducing
8. off	around	round

UNIT 9 Machines

1 Choose the correct option.

a. A machine is something that helps us do work with *less* / *more* effort.

b. Simple machines have ***few or no*** / ***many*** moving parts.

c. Simple machines were defined by Renaissance scientists over ***200*** / ***500*** years ago.

d. We can combine ***complex*** / ***simple*** machines to make ***complex*** / ***simple*** machines.

2 Write the simple machine and match it to the correct definition.

Simple machine

wedge ____ [e]

____ [ ]

____ [ ]

____ [ ]

____ [ ]

____ [ ]

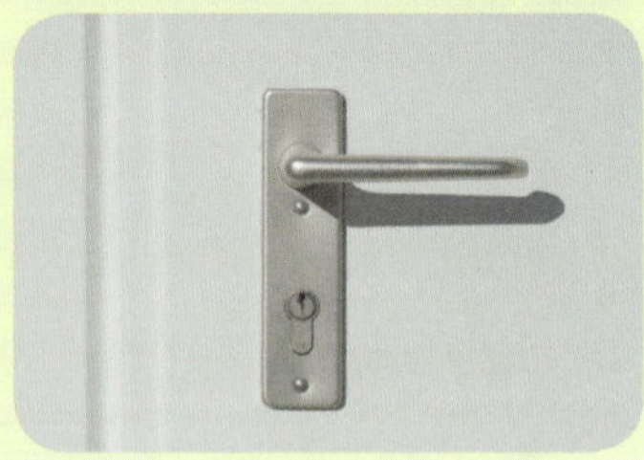

Definitions

a. It is an inclined plane which goes around a cylinder or cone. We use it to hold things together or lift objects.
b. It has a wheel, an axle and a rope. We use it to lift, lower or move objects.
c. It has one or more wheels which move around an axle. We use it to move things more easily.
d. It is a flat, slanting surface. It is used to connect a lower level to a higher level.
e. This machine has one or two slanting surfaces. We use it to cut or separate material.
f. This is a rigid bar which is placed on a support called a fulcrum. We use it to lift objects.

3 Identify the class of lever and complete the definition.

a

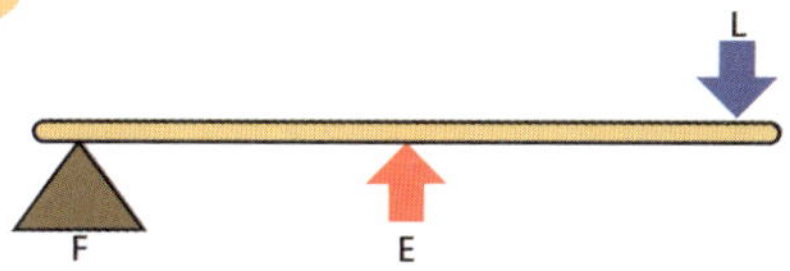

Class ________ levers

The fulcrum is at one end.

The ____________________

is between the fulcrum and the load.

b

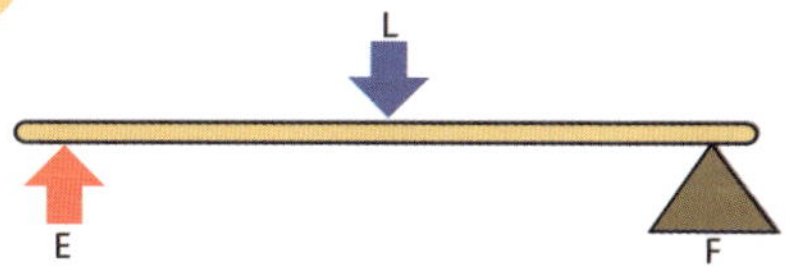

Class ________ levers

The ____________________

is between the effort and the fulcrum.

c

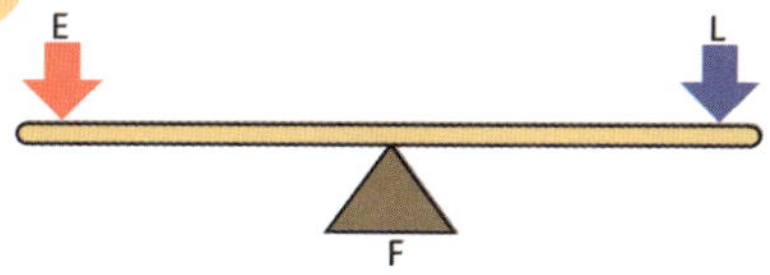

Class ________ levers

The ____________________

is between the effort and the load.

4 Identify the type of lever.

a

Class ________ lever

b

Class ________ lever

c

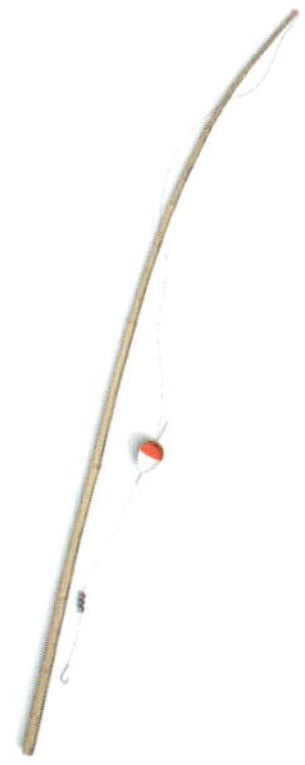

Class ________ lever

5 Identify the simple machines in the tin opener.

a. The handles are *levers*.

b. The key is a w____________________.

c. A s____________________ holds the tin opener together.

d. The blade which cuts the tin is a w____________________.

6 Complete the sentences about energy.

function	forms	sources	electricity supply
around	~~energy~~	cannot	batteries

a. Machines need ___energy___ to work.

b. Energy can take a variety of ______________ such as light, heat and sound.

c. We ______________ see it or touch it but is it all ______________ us.

d. Energy comes from different ______________ like people, wind, water or fuel.

e. Many complex machines need electricity to work. This can come from ______________ or from an ______________.

f. We can also classify machines by their ______________.

7 Circle the energy source the machines use.

a

wind
electricity
(people)

b

fuel
water
wind

c

people
electricity
water

d

wind
electricity
people

e

fuel
electricity
water

f

fuel
electricity supply
batteries

8 Use the information in two boxes to write true sentences about the functions of machines.

... have a motor or an engine. They ...	... make things ...	... are used for communication ...
... hot or cold.	... and making calculations.	... use electricity or fuel to make things move.

a. *Mechanical machines ...* ________________________.

b. *Thermal machines ...* ________________________.

c. *Information processing machines ...* ________________________.

9 Identify the functions of the machines.

a

b

c
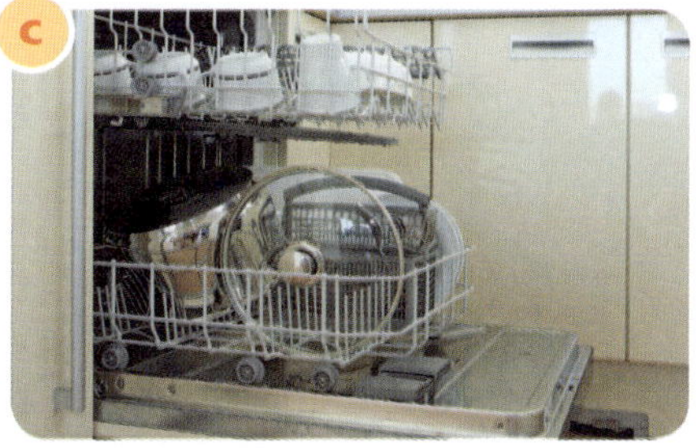

10 Match and write true sentences about safety when working with tools.

Roll up long	is a possibility something could enter your eyes.
Wear safety goggles when there	with a tool in your hand.
Never run	sleeves and tie back long hair.

a. ________________________

b. ________________________

c. ________________________

Find out at home!

1 Experiment with a lever:

1. Make a first class lever:
   - Tape a marker onto a table so that it does not move.
   - Place a ruler on top.
2. Place a rubber on one end of the lever. Place coins on the other end of the lever so that they lift the rubber. Add the information to the chart below.
3. Experiment moving the ruler so that the marker is at different distances from the rubber. Complete the chart below.

Distance of marker from rubber	Number of coins needed to lift rubber

2 Complete the sentences.

a. When the fulcrum is near the load, ________.

b. When the fulcrum is near the effort, ________.

c. In this experiment, the fulcrum is ________.

d. In this experiment, the load ________.

e. In this experiment, the effort ________.

Skills check

1. Read the information about a class at a local museum. Complete the notes.

Do you like science?
Are you an inventor?

If you are between 8 and 14 years old, you are invited to attend a beginner's engineering class.

We will:

- learn about simple and complex machines
- learn about how we can use renewable energy sources
- carry out experiments
- have a great time

Price: €10
Saturday 20 April
10.00 – 12.00

MUNICIPAL SCIENCE MUSEUM

Hi! Shall we go to the engineering class together? My mum can take us home but we will have to take the bus there. See you tomorrow!
Carol

Notes	
1. Place:	*Municipal Science Museum*
2. Day:	
3. Price:	
4. Travel there by:	
5. Go with:	
6. Age of participants:	

Glossary

English	Your language	English	Your language

Unit 1: Body systems

English	Your language	English	Your language
circulatory system (n)		digestive system (n)	
heart (n)		stomach (n)	
blood vessels (n)		small intestine (n)	
excretory system (n)		large intestine (n)	
kidneys (n)		nervous system (n)	
urine (n)		smell (n)	
ureters (n)		taste (n)	
bladder (n)		sight (n)	
urethra (n)		hearing (n)	
respiratory system (n)		skeleton (n)	
		joints (n)	
trachea (n)		muscles (n)	
diaphragm (n)		reproductive system (n)	

Unit 2: Looking after yourself

English	Your language	English	Your language
hygienic (adj)		healthy (adj)	
vaccination (n)		exercise (n)	
check-up (n)		memory (n)	
X-ray (n)		infectious (adj)	
ultrasound machine (n)		disease (n)	
		pathogen (n)	
microsurgery (n)		weight gain (n)	
antibiotics (n)			
endorphins (n)		sleep loss (n)	
plaque (n)			
additive (n)		headache (n)	
white blood cells (n)		backache (n)	
		eye strain (n)	
red blood cells (n)		pollen (n)	
		dust (n)	
empathy (n)		alcohol (n)	
empathise (v)		drugs (n)	
emotions (n)			

Glossary

English	Your language	English	Your language

Unit 3: Living things

English	Your language	English	Your language
cell (n)		Animal Kingdom (n)	
interact (v)			
tissue (n)		Plant Kingdom (n)	
organ (n)			
organism (n)		yeast (n)	
interaction (n)		decomposer (n)	
nutrition (n)		environment (n)	
reproduction (n)		nutrients (n)	
respiration (n)		seeds (n)	
excretion (n)		sweat (n)	
growth (n)		urine (n)	
movement (n)		bacteria (n)	
Monera Kingdom (n)		unicellular (adj)	
		multicellular (adj)	
Protist Kingdom (n)		mould (n)	
		algae (n)	
Fungus Kingdom (n)			

Unit 4: Animals

English	Your language	English	Your language
vertebrate (n)		thorax (n)	
invertebrate (n)		cephalothorax (n)	
carnivore (n)		beak (n)	
omnivore (n)		meat (n)	
herbivore (n)		digest (v)	
oviparous (adj)		swallow (v)	
viviparous (adj)		pharynx (n)	
ovoviviparous (adj)		trachea (n)	
consumer (n)		nostril (n)	
ruminant (n)		moist (adj)	
chew (v)		aquatic (adj)	
gill (n)		offspring (n)	
capillaries (n)		nest (n)	
frogspawn (n)		den (n)	
extinct (adj)		segmented (adj)	
abdomen (n)		antennae (n)	
exoskeleton (n)		wings (n)	

Glossary

Unit 5: Plants

English	Your language	English	Your language
grass (n)	________	carpel (n)	________
bush (n)	________	stigma (n)	________
stem (n)	________	ovary (n)	________
roots (n)	________	pollination (n)	________
fruit (n)	________	herbaceous (adj)	________
leaves (n)	________	deciduous (adj)	________
photosynthesis (n)	________	evergreen (adj)	________
light (n)	________	branch (n)	________
energy (n)	________	thorns (n)	________
carbon dioxide (n)	________	cone (n)	________
minerals (n)	________	mosses (n)	________
flowering (adj)	________	ferns (n)	________
non-flowering (adj)	________	angiosperm (n)	________
petals (n)	________	gymnosperm (n)	________
stamen (n)	________	spore (n)	________
pollen (n)	________		

English	Your language	English	Your language

Unit 6: Ecosystems

English	Your language	English	Your language
ecosystem (n)	______	population (n)	______
living thing (n)	______	community (n)	______
	______	habitat (n)	______
non-living thing (n)	______	producer (n)	______
	______	consumer (n)	______
desert (n)	______	primary consumer (n)	______
forest (n)	______		______
grassland (n)	______	secondary consumer (n)	______
mountain (n)	______		______
ocean (n)	______	decomposer (n)	______
shoreline (n)	______	tertiary consumer (n)	______
coral reef (n)	______		______
	______	food chain (n)	______
nature reserve (n)	______		______
	______	food web (n)	______
mollusc (n)	______		______
litter (n)	______	predator (n)	______
hooked (adj)	______	prey (n)	______
flamingo (n)	______	savannah (n)	______
fauna (n)	______	temperate (adj)	______
flora (n)	______		

Glossary

Unit 7: Matter, materials and forces

English	Your language	English	Your language
reversible (adj)		density (n)	
irreversible (adj)		physical change (n)	
fragile (adj)			
transparent (adj)		chemical change (n)	
opaque (adj)			
resistant (adj)		solid (n)	
rigid (adj)		liquid (n)	
dissolve (v)		gas (n)	
bioplastics (n)		state (n)	
mass (n)		combustion (n)	
volume (n)		oxidation (n)	
gravity (n)		putrefaction (n)	
magnetism (n)		homogeneous (adj)	
friction (n)		heterogeneous (adj)	
buoyancy (n)		sieving (n)	
elastic (adj)		filtration (n)	
non-elastic (adj)		evaporation (n)	
float (v)		crystals (n)	

Unit 8: Energy

English	Your language
renewable (adj)	
non-renewable (adj)	
wind farm (n)	
pollution (n)	
acid rain (n)	
temperature (n)	
ice caps (n)	
fossil fuels (n)	
oil (n)	
coal (n)	
gas (n)	
kinetic energy (n)	
electrical energy (n)	

English	Your language
light energy (n)	
thermal energy (n)	
sound energy (n)	
chemical energy (n)	
vibrations (n)	
solar energy (n)	
wind energy (n)	
hydropower (n)	
light source (n)	
translucent (adj)	

Glossary

English	Your language	English	Your language

Unit 9: Machines

English	Your language	English	Your language
wheel and axle (n)	______	safety (n)	______
	______	electrical charge (n)	______
screw (n)	______		______
lever (n)	______	electrical conductor (n)	______
pulley (n)	______		______
wedge (n)	______	electrical insulator (n)	______
inclined plane (n)	______		______
	______	current electricity (n)	______
slanting (adj)	______		______
fulcrum (n)	______	static electricity (n)	______
load (n)	______		______
effort (n)	______	electrical circuit (n)	______
petrol (n)	______		______
fuel (n)	______	generator (n)	______
battery (n)	______	conductor (n)	______
plug (n)	______	electrical component (n)	______
socket (n)	______		______
motor (n)	______	switch (n)	______